GROWING UP

THE MACMILLAN COMPANY
NEW YORK · BOSTON · CHICAGO
DALLAS · ATLANTA · SAN FRANCISCO

MACMILLAN AND CO., LIMITED
LONDON · BOMBAY · CALCUTTA
MADRAS · MELBOURNE

THE MACMILLAN COMPANY
OF CANADA, LIMITED
TORONTO

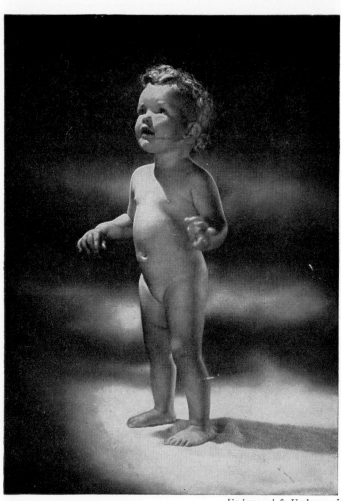

Growing Up

*The Story of How We
Become Alive, Are Born
And Grow Up*

by

Karl de Schweinitz

**SECOND EDITION
REVISED**

1950

New York: The Macmillan Company

SET UP BY BROWN BROTHERS LINOTYPERS
PRINTED IN THE UNITED STATES OF AMERICA

GROWING UP

THIS book tells how we become alive, and are born and grow up.

It is a story that has happened to everybody, to your neighbors next door, to your mother and to your father, and to you.

We are all interested in it. We have all been babies and we have all been born, so, of course, we want to know how we came into the world.

It is to tell boys and girls this story that I have written Growing Up.

CONTENTS

ILLUSTRATIONS

GROWING TO BE A BABY

CHAPTER I

GROWING TO BE A BABY

WHEN you came into the world you were a baby, but you had not always been a baby. Before you could be born you had first to grow to be a baby.

That meant a great deal of growing, for when you began your life you were much smaller than you were on the day on which you were born. You were so small that you could hardly have been seen. You were smaller than the tiniest dot that you can make with the sharpest pencil you can find. You were smaller than the little specks that dance in a sunbeam where it comes through the window. You were so small that you did not even seem to be a baby, and you really weren't a baby. You were almost as round as a ball and you looked more like a little egg than like anything else; and that is exactly what you were— a tiny, little egg.

It was from this little egg that you grew to be a baby. That is how we all start living. The tallest and biggest man you know began his life as a tiny egg. Your parents and your grandparents and the rest of the people on the earth started growing in this way, and so did you. You came into the world as a baby but before you were born you grew to be a baby from a tiny, little egg.

Drawing by Eleanor M. Paxson.

This little white spot on this page is ten times larger than the egg from which you started growing.

WHERE EGGS GROW

Chapter II

WHERE EGGS GROW

Lions, elephants, dogs, horses, alligators, fish, robins, chickens, frogs all begin their lives in the same way that you did. They start as tiny eggs.

Even trees, carrots, roses, lilies, and other plants grow from eggs, that is, they grow from seeds and the seeds grow from eggs. The poppy seeds, the sunflower seeds, the hollyhock seeds, and the other seeds that we plant in the garden have grown to be seeds from little eggs.

When the eggs of the plants first begin growing they are quite small, too small to be seen even with sharp eyes. They are in the flowers and the blossoms, usually just above where the petals join the stem. Here there is a little place called the ovary, and in the ovary are the eggs.

If you pull the ovary apart very carefully

you may see tiny bumps growing from its sides. These are the eggs.

Most of the plants you know each have at least one flower, and most of the flowers you know each have at least one ovary. The blossoms of the trees—the apple blossom, the cherry blossom, and all the other blossoms, are the flowers of the trees. At the bottom of the flower or blossom is the little place, called the ovary, which holds the eggs.

The eggs grow until they have become seeds. Then they stop growing. Before they can start growing again they must be placed in the ground. Sometimes we speak of the ground as mother earth. The earth is the great mother in the body of which seeds begin to grow to be plants—flowers, vegetables, trees, and grain.

The water, like the earth, is mother to many growing things. It is here that the eggs of most fish grow up.

If you have eaten shad roe you may have noticed the little round balls, each about as big as the head of a pin. These little balls are the eggs of the shad.

In the springtime, and in some parts of the

Photograph by J. Fletcher Street.

Jack-in-the-pulpit. Jack is the flower. The pulpit is really a leaf. The ovary is inside the flower at about where Jack and the pulpit join the stem of the plant.

Photograph by H. Armstrong Roberts.

Apple trees in bloom. At the bottom of each blossom or flower is the ovary with the eggs that will soon grow to be seeds of the apple.

world even earlier, the mother shad leaves the ocean where she lives and swims up one of the rivers that empties into it. She swims sometimes for more than one hundred miles until she has left the salt water behind her and has

Courtesy of United States Bureau of Fisheries.
Eggs of salmon. They are among the largest of fish eggs.

reached the fresh water as it flows toward the sea. There she finds a place where the stream is shallow and quiet and where the sun takes the chill from the water. Here she lays her eggs. They have been staying in her ovaries—she has two ovaries—just as the eggs of the plants stay in the ovaries of the flowers. But, instead of being placed in the ground like the seeds, the eggs of the shad are sent into the water by the mother through an opening underneath her body.

After the shad has laid her eggs she swims away and forgets all about them. From four to seven days later each egg has become something that looks very much like a tiny fish, and in three or four weeks it has grown to be a little shad, about an inch long, which can swim about and take care of itself.

Birds and chickens grow from eggs like the fish and the plants, but instead of growing in the water or in the ground they grow in a nest. The hen has an ovary in her body. There the egg stays until the time comes for it to be laid. Then it moves down through a long pipe or tube, growing a little bit as it goes, and passes out of the hen through an opening under her tail feathers, and drops into the nest.

The hen keeps the egg warm by sitting on the nest and the egg begins to grow very fast. In three weeks it has become a tiny chick which breaks the shell that once protected the egg and comes out into the nest, a fuzzy little fellow.

This is the way in which robins and sparrows and other birds are born.

The dog, the elephant, the mouse, and the other four-legged animals grow from eggs but

Photograph by Eugene J. Hall.
Just four hours out of the shell.

they do not grow in the ground or in the water. They grow up in the nest but the nest is not in the trees or in the bushes or in the grass. It is in the body of the mother. When the egg leaves the ovary it does not pass out of the mother. It goes close by into a little bag, called the uterus. The uterus is the nest in which the egg grows

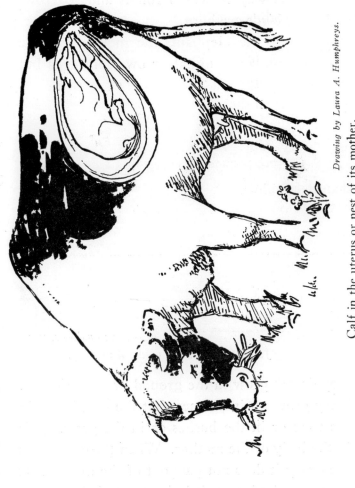

Drawing by Laura A. Humphreys.

Calf in the uterus or nest of its mother.

to be a mouse or an elephant or a dog or whatever other animal the mother happens to be.

This, also, is the way in which human babies grow. The eggs from which they come stay in ovaries just as the eggs of the plants and of the fish and the birds and the four-legged animals do. Every baby's mother has two ovaries inside her body. They are very small, not much thicker than her thumbs.

When the egg leaves its ovary it goes into the bag or nest, called the uterus. Sometimes the uterus is called the womb. It is near the ovaries, and is in the very middle of the body of the baby's mother but quite low down, even below where the stomach is. It is here that the egg grows to be a baby.

What better place could there be in which to grow? The seeds in the ground can be disturbed by anybody who digs into the flower beds. The eggs in the water can be washed ashore and hurt in storms, and you have often seen birds' eggs that have been broken by being blown out of the nest. But nothing like this can happen to the egg that is growing to be a baby. In the body,

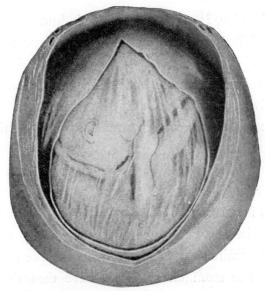

After De Lee. Courtesy of W. B. Saunders Company.
Baby in the uterus or nest of its mother.

of its mother it is always safe and comfortable and warm.

This is where you started your life and this is where everybody who has lived began living. When you were a tiny egg you had the best place in all the world to grow—a little nest in the body of your mother.

Eggs of a red-winged blackbird in their nest.

POLLEN AND SPERM

CHAPTER III

POLLEN AND SPERM

BEFORE an egg can become an animal or a plant it must be helped to start growing. It cannot start by itself.

The little eggs in the ovaries of the flowers would wither and die if something that we call pollen did not join them and help them to become seeds.

Pollen is the yellow powder that you sometimes find on the tip of your nose after you have tried to smell a snapdragon or a dandelion or a lily. Nearly every flower has pollen.

The next time you see an Easter lily look at it carefully and you will notice, growing out of the middle of the flower, a tall thread or stem. This stem leads to the ovary of the lily. It is called the pistil. Growing up around the pistil, but not quite so tall as it is, are six threads or stems. On the top of each of these stems is a little sack full of pollen.

Pollen is usually yellow. It is so light that it scarcely weighs anything at all. A tiny puff of wind can blow it away. It sticks to whatever touches it just as flour does. If an insect comes too near the pollen it is almost sure to get some of it on its body.

There is a certain kind of moth that is very fond of visiting the Easter lily. When this moth flies into the lily it brushes against the pollen and the pollen sticks to its shoulders. Then when the moth visits another lily it carries the pollen with it. As it enters this lily it passes the tall pistil that leads to the ovary. The top of the pistil is sticky and it catches some of the pollen from the body of the moth.

No sooner does the pollen reach the top of the pistil than it begins to grow. The pistil is hollow. From each grain of pollen a tiny thread grows down through the pistil into the ovary of the lily. There are the little eggs. Into each egg a thread from a grain of pollen goes and becomes a part of the egg, and the egg

Photograph by Theodore H. Lueders.

Easter Lily. Count six dark tops growing on thread-like stems (the stamens). This is the yellow pollen. The longest thread with the white knobby top is the pistil. It leads to the ovary inside the lily just above where the flower joins the stem.

A butterfly visiting phlox. When the butterfly leaves this flower it will carry pollen with it to another flower.

and the pollen together start growing to be a seed.

This is how the eggs of the flowers and the blossoms begin growing. The wind, or the bees and the butterflies and the moths and other insects, carry the pollen from one flower or blossom to another flower or blossom—from one lily to another lily, from one rose to another rose, and so on. As soon as a grain of pollen touches the top of the pistil it starts growing down through it into the ovary where it enters one of the little eggs and becomes part of it. The pollen and the egg together form the seed. By itself the pollen could not grow to be a seed. The egg needs the pollen and the pollen needs the egg. It is when they join together that they begin to grow to be a seed.

There are some flowers which have only pollen and there are some flowers which have only eggs, but most flowers have both pollen and eggs. Almost always the pollen that joins the eggs comes from another flower—that is, from another flower of the same kind. The flower from which the pollen goes might be called the father, and the flower to which the pollen is carried might be called the mother, so that every seed can be said to have had a mother and a father.

There is something like pollen that starts the eggs of animals growing. This is a very little creature with a very long name. The name is spermatazoön. We shall call it sperm. The sperm is like an animal. It can move. It looks a little bit like the pollywogs that you see in brooks and ponds in the springtime. It seems to be all head and tail, a round little head or body and a very, very long tail. The sperm is much smaller than the eggs. It is so tiny that you would not be able to see one sperm alone no matter how sharp your eyes might be.

But although one sperm by itself is too small to be seen it is possible for you to see what one million or more sperms crowded together look like. The next time you have fish for dinner, ask your mother whether you cannot watch while the fish is split open and cleaned and prepared for cooking. You will find inside the fish either the roe with its thousands of little eggs or something that looks like the roe but

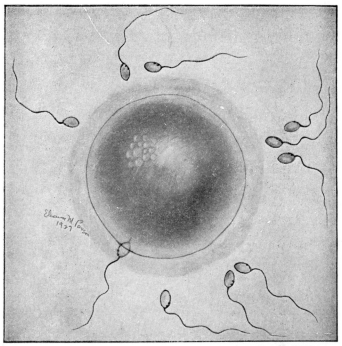

Drawing by Eleanor M. Paxson.

Sperms of the minnow swimming to the egg.

The sperms and the egg in this picture have been drawn many times larger than the sperms and the egg of this fish really are.

which is smoother and softer. This is the milt.
It is a kind of jelly with millions of sperms
in it.

The fish in which you find the eggs or roe is
the mother fish. The fish in which you find the
sperms or milt is the father fish. It is the milt
or sperms of the father fish that starts the eggs of
the mother fish growing.

When the mother or roe shad swims away
from the ocean and up into the fresh water she
does not swim alone. Hundreds of other roe
shad swim with her. The roe shad swim until
they find the father or buck shad, hundreds of
which have gone up the river ahead of them.
Then from an opening underneath her body
each mother shad sends her eggs into the water.
The father shad swims immediately after her
and sends out over the eggs a liquid that looks
very much like skimmed milk. It is alive with
sperms that are too small to be seen.

As soon as a sperm meets an egg it swims right
into it. The tail of the sperm drops off and stays
outside the egg, but the rest of the sperm joins
with the egg just as the pollen from one flower
joins the egg of another flower, and together

the egg and the sperm start growing to be a baby fish.

Some fish hollow out little nests in the bottom of rivers and other waters and in these nests they start their eggs growing.

With sun fish it is the father who makes the nest. He finds a sandy spot in shallow water. He pushes and pulls the bigger pebbles to the outside of the nest and sweeps it clean with his fins. Looking into the stream you would then see a little scooped out place. This is where the baby sun fish will be hatched.

The father fish now swims away to find a female or roe sun fish. His body becomes brighter as if to attract the roe fish. When he meets one he swims about her inviting her to follow him. They go to the nest. When they reach it they swim toward each other stopping just over the nest. Their bodies touch each other and as they do so the mother sun fish sends the eggs into the water and the father fish sends out the sperms. The sperms join the eggs and the baby fish start growing

The father fish then usually drives the mother

Photograph by H. Armstrong Roberts.

Mother pig.

fish away and it is he who watches over the eggs until the little fish are hatched.

For the sperm to join the egg in the water is not the safest way to start a baby growing. There must be many eggs and many sperms that do not meet, and if they do not meet almost immediately the sperms die, for the sperms cannot live in the water longer than three minutes.

The sperms of chickens and other birds are less likely to be lost than are the sperms of fish. The rooster places them inside the body of the hen where nothing can harm them and where they can easily find the eggs. If you have ever lived on a farm you may have seen the rooster doing this, but if you did not understand what was happening you might have thought that the rooster and the hen were fighting.

The rooster flies up on the back of the hen. While he is there an opening under his tail feathers touches an opening under the tail feathers of the hen. The rooster can then send the sperms into the body of the hen without the same danger of losing them that the shad face when they send their sperms into the water.

As soon as the sperms have left the rooster they go up through the hen until they meet the egg as it leaves the ovary. The hard shell which we must break when we eat an egg has not yet formed about it and one of the sperms—only one —succeeds in entering the egg. The tail of the sperm drops off and stays outside but the rest of the sperm joins the egg. The egg with the help of the sperm now starts growing, and if, after it is laid, it is kept warm it will keep on growing, until it has become a little chicken.

The dog, the lion, the horse, the pig place their sperms in the body of the mother in much the same way that the rooster does but the sperms instead of going through an opening as they do with the rooster pass from these animals through a little pipe or tube that is on the outside of the body. This little pipe or tube is called the penis. When the male animal sends the sperms to the female he seems to be trying to climb on to her back. As he does this the penis fits into an opening in her body. This is the opening of what we call the vagina, and it is through the vagina of the mother that the sperms go when they leave the father.

Photograph by J. Fletcher Street.

Dog sitting for his picture.

While the sperms are still living in the male animal they stay in two oval-shaped places called testicles. The testicles are held in a little bag outside the body and under the penis. It is also through the penis that the urine or waste water passes.

The sperms of men, like those of the four-legged animals, live in two testicles in a little bag under the penis. The father places the sperms in the body of the mother in very much the same way that the four-legged animals do, only the mother and father can lie together facing each other. The penis then fits into the vagina of the mother which has its own opening underneath the opening for the urine or waste water.

*Photograph by
Howard Gosner.*

Human
Sperms.

These little sperms are hundreds of times larger than the real living sperms.

When the sperms leave the father they are in a liquid, called semen, that is a little thicker than milk and that looks something like milk. The sperms are so tiny that hundreds of them can live in one drop of semen.

As soon as the semen has entered the mother the sperms start swimming toward the egg as it comes from the ovary. The sperm that meets the egg joins it and together the sperm and the egg start growing to be a baby.

This is the way that you began your life. The egg was not you and the sperm was not you. It was when they came together that you became alive. People everywhere begin their lives in this way. Like the fish and the birds and the beasts, we all start to be ourselves when the sperm joins the egg.

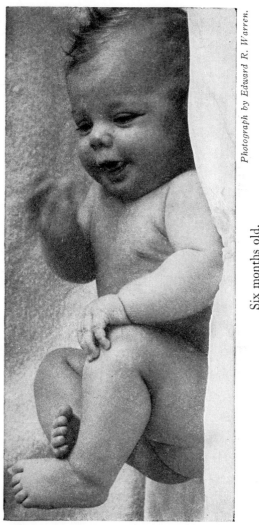

Photograph by Edward R. Warren.

Six months old.

FROM AN EGG TO A BABY

CHAPTER IV

FROM AN EGG TO A BABY

THE egg from which you came was one of thousands of eggs in the ovaries of your mother and the sperm from which you came was one of millions of sperms in the testicles of your father. Once each month an egg leaves one of the ovaries of the mother and goes to the uterus. If when it is in the uterus or on its way there a sperm joins it, the two together—egg and sperm—start growing to be a baby. If no sperms have been sent to meet it the egg stays in the uterus for a little while and then passes out through the vagina. It is so tiny that the mother does not even know that it has left her.

You began your life because the sperm found the egg. The moment they joined each other you started growing. You grew very fast. Your shape changed. You began to have a place for your stomach and another place for your heart and lungs. Then the beginnings of your head and arms and legs showed themselves.

At the end of about one month you looked something like a tiny curled up fish. You were still so small that your whole body could have rested on the nail of your mother's little finger; but you kept on growing.

Another month passed. You were now more than an inch tall and you began to look like a little baby.

After four months had passed, your mother felt you stirring in her body. She now knew that you were alive and that after a few more months you would be ready to be born.

While you were doing all this growing you needed food. At first you were fed in somewhat the same way that a chick is fed when it is growing in the shell. Your egg fed you. Only a small part of an egg, called the nucleus, grows. The rest is chiefly food for the growing part. The growing part soaks the food up into itself very much as a sponge or a washcloth soaks up water.

After you had used all the food in your egg

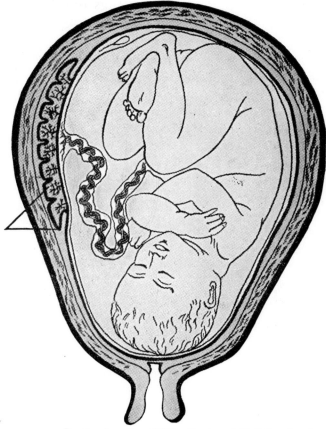

Prentiss-Arey after Ahlfeld.   Courtesy of W. B. Saunders Co.
The baby in the uterus with the cord through which it
is fed from the body of its mother.

you were fed by your mother. A long cord grew from your body. Through this cord ran three tiny tubes ending in a kind of sponge. This sponge took from your mother the food you needed to help you grow. Perhaps you have noticed a little curled dent, called the navel, near your stomach. That is where the cord entered your body.

All this time you were living in the uterus of your mother. When you first entered the uterus it was very small, not much bigger than a pear, but as you grew the sides of the uterus stretched to make room for you. Your mother's whole body became larger so that it could take better care of you. Her breasts grew bigger so that they could fill with milk for you to draw from them after your birth.

When you had been growing for nine months you were ready to be born. You were lying in the uterus all curled up like a little kitten asleep. The time had come for you to leave your mother.

The sides of the uterus now stopped stretching. Instead they began to push and to squeeze the baby out. Usually the baby lies with its head pointing downward toward the tube called the vagina which leads to the outside of the mother's body. The vagina is narrow but it stretches as the baby enters it. Slowly the baby passes from the uterus and into the world, going out by the same opening through which nine months before the sperm had gone in. Some babies need a whole day or more in which to make this journey and some babies are born in a few minutes. Perhaps your mother will tell you how long you took to be born.

The pushing and the stretching that the body must do to help the baby to leave the uterus uses up the mother's strength. It is hard work for her—the doctors call it labor. She either goes to a hospital or calls a doctor and a nurse to her home. They take care of her and of the new born baby. The doctor cuts the cord through which the food had been going from the mother to the baby, and from now on the baby will feed through its mouth.

The doctor listened eagerly for the first little cry that you made after you were born for then he knew that you were alive; but your mother

Courtesy of the Philadelphia Child Health Society.

Mother feeding her baby.

and your father were happiest of all, for after having waited nine months for you to grow to be a baby they could now at last see you and hold you in their arms.

ANIMALS AND BABIES

CHAPTER V

ANIMALS AND BABIES

ALL the animals that start their lives in the
bodies of their mothers grow from eggs in the
same way that you did. Some of the animals
take more time to do this than you needed. Most
of them take less time.

A baby spends nine months in the body of its
mother. An elephant spends twenty months there
and a mouse spends twenty days. A horse needs
a little more than eleven months in which to
get ready to be born and a rabbit needs only one
month. But the rabbit and the horse and the
mouse and the elephant all grow up in the bodies
of their mothers just as babies do, and they are
born just as babies are born.

Usually babies grow one at a time. Now and
then two babies—twins—will grow in the body
of the mother and once in a long, long while

there will be a mother who will have triplets, that is three babies at a birth. There have even been quintuplets, that is, five babies born at one birth.

Only a few animals, generally the larger ones like the elephant and the horse and the cow, grow alone in the body of the mother. Most animals are born in litters, that is two, three, six, ten or even fourteen or more are born one after another of the same mother at the same birth. From three to eight puppies and from three to six kittens are the usual number of babies that dogs and cats have, and often as many as fourteen little pigs will be born in the same litter.

At the beginning of their lives animals and babies are so nearly alike that you could not tell them one from the other. If you were to see the egg of a baby and the egg of an elephant and of a mouse you would not know which was which. A rabbit that has been growing for a week seems so much like a baby that has been growing for three or four weeks that it would be hard for you to tell them apart. But the longer that animals and babies grow the more different from each other they become.

A mother dog feeding her litter of puppies.

Animals are much stronger and much better able to take care of themselves when they come into the world than babies are, and after they are born they grow up much more quickly than babies do.

Animals can use their legs earlier than babies can. A colt or a calf can stand on its feet on the same day on which it is born. The giraffe can stand up within twenty minutes after it has left its mother's body. But most babies cannot stand before they are a year old.

Young animals can eat the same things that grown-up animals eat long before babies can eat the things that grown-up people eat. As soon as babies are born they are fed with milk from their mothers' breasts. If a mother cannot feed a baby with her own milk she uses the milk of the cow and for nearly a year milk is the chief food of the baby.

The animals that grow up in the bodies of their mothers are fed with milk by their mothers in the same way that babies are fed. We call these animals mammals. Mice, lions, dogs, cats, men, women, are mammals. The name is easy to remember because it sounds so much like

Buffalo calf drinking its mother's milk.

The little giraffe standing beside its mother is only
two days old.

mamma. Milk from the mother's breast is the first food of all mammals, but most of the four-legged animals soon start eating other things. The milk that is brought every day to our homes is the milk that the cow has for her calf, but when we drink it we are not harming the calf for he needs only a little of his mother's milk.

The animals do not need to be taken care of by their mothers and fathers for nearly so long a time as babies do. Many young animals do not even see their fathers. The little care they must have is given to them by the mother, and the father wanders away and forgets all about his family. There are some animal fathers, how-ever, that stay with their children and help the mother to show them how to find their food. The lion helps the lioness to teach the baby lion how to hunt, but before the young lion is two years old he is a skilful enough hunter to find his own food and to take care of himself. Horses, cows, and dogs usually have grown to be as big as their parents by the time they are two years old. Rabbits are full grown in less than a year and nearly all these animals do not need the care of their mothers for more than a few weeks. At the end of a month and a half a mouse is large enough and strong enough to have babies of its own.

But at two years of age a boy or girl could not live if its parents did not take care of it all the time. A lion, two years old, can roam for miles and miles through the forest, hunting its food. A baby, two years old, would be lost in five minutes if it toddled away from home.

Although children have done a great deal of growing by the time they are two years old they are then really only at the beginning of their growing. Each year they become a little bit bigger and heavier and taller and stronger.

While their bodies are growing their minds are growing too. They learn how to talk and how to think, how to use tools, how to read and how to write. It is a long, long time before they are grown up and can begin to have babies of their own.

They keep on growing and learning after the animals have stopped growing and learning, and they become wiser than any of the animals and can do many things that the animals cannot do. But babies and animals are born in the same

Lion Cub.

This baby lion is only three and a half months old, but what
a sturdy little fellow he is.

way and start their lives in the same way, and, although when they are grown up they are very different from each other, if you were to see them as tiny little eggs you could not tell them apart.

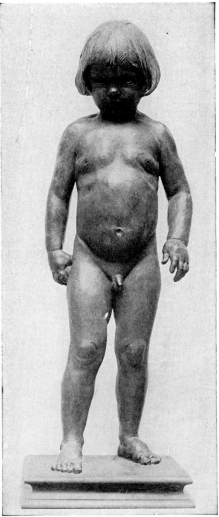

Man Cub, a bronze statue by
Alexander Stirling Calder.

MATING

CHAPTER VI

MATING

BEFORE you started growing to be a baby, your
mother and your father had met and loved each
other and mated. Ever since they had grown up
they had each been looking for a mate, that is,
for some one to love and to marry and with
whom to have children. They may not have
known that they were doing this, but they were.
That is what we all do as soon as we are grown.
Each of us, although usually not knowing it,
looks for his or her mate, for some one to love
and to join with in having a baby; some one with
whom to share a home in which the baby, after
it is born, can grow up.

Birds and animals mate. Plants do not mate.
Plants cannot go to each other. They cannot
themselves send the pollen to the egg. Their
pollen is carried by the wind and the bees and
other flying creatures. But many flowers and

blossoms have colors and perfumes that make the bees and the other insects want to come to them.

The moths like the pure white petals of the lily and so they fly to it. The bees like the red rose and the white rose and so they visit the roses, and as the moths and the bees go from flower to flower they carry from one lily to another lily, from one rose to another rose, the pollen that joins with the egg in growing to be a seed.

It is when the eggs are ready for the pollen and the pollen is ready for the eggs that the flowers show their most charming colors. They fill the air with their perfume and in the gardens, the meadows, and the woods the butterflies and the bees and the other insects fly from plant to plant and from blossom to blossom. This is the most beautiful time of the spring and the summer, the time when the pollen is being carried from flower to flower and when with it the eggs are starting to grow to be seeds.

This, too, is the time when the birds sing most of all. Many of the songs you hear are their love songs. Cock robin whose voice is one of the first that people in the north hear after the snow has

Photograph by J. Fletcher Street.

Flowers in a Garden.

Photograph by H. Armstrong Roberts.

Crowing Rooster.

left the ground is silent when he is in the south. But when he reaches the north the time for his mating has come and he sings to the hen robin.

It is then, also, that the birds like to show their bright colors. It is when the peacock is seeking a mate that he opens his wonderful feathers, blue and green and shining purple. It is when the turkey gobbler wants the turkey hen to mate with him that he raises his tail feathers like a fan and gives his gobble call while his wing feathers spread until they scrape the ground.

It is at the time of mating that the antlers or horns of the stag have grown to their greatest size. It is then that the bodies of many fish become brighter and more beautiful. It is then that the call of the cow moose and the answering call of the bull moose can be heard in the woods. Every animal has some way of being attractive and of making love to its mate, and much of all that is beautiful on earth is the beauty of the animals when they are mating and the beauty of the flowers when they are being visited by the bees and the other flying creatures.

For some animals the time of mating is in the

spring; for some it is in the fall. For some
animals it is twice a year, for others even more
often, but whenever the time comes for the sperm
to join the egg an animal will usually take as
his mate the first animal of his kind that he sees.
The animals do not know that when they join
together a baby animal may start growing. They
only know that they feel like doing this just as
sometimes they feel like eating and at other times
like sleeping; and if after the sperm has joined
the egg two animals keep on living together it
is not because they know that soon they will
become parents.

Only people know how babies are born and
they are the only creatures that plan to live together and have children. People do not choose
as their mates the first persons they meet after
having grown up. Each man and each woman
wants to marry some one whom he or she can
love, and rather than marry without love, some
people never marry at all.

That is one of the ways in which men and
women are different from the animals. Men and
women know that when the sperm joins the egg
a baby will start growing, and when they mate,

When the peacock is seeking a mate he opens his wonderful feathers, blue and green and shining purple.

Bull Moose and His Mate.

each wants to mate with the person he or she loves. The world is full of things that tell of the love and mating of men and women. Many pictures and statues, many of the songs we sing and much of our music is about love, and so are many of our favorite tales, like the Sleeping Beauty and Cinderella.

It is love and mating that make growing and being born the most interesting of all stories. What better way could there be for you to have begun your life than to have had a mother and a father who loved each other so much that they mated and started you growing to be a baby.

Bathing Girl, a statue in bronze by
Edmund Austin Stewardson.

YOUR STORY AND MY STORY

CHAPTER VII

YOUR STORY AND MY STORY

Now we have come to the end of this story about how we become alive, and are born, and grow up.

It is a story that has happened to each one of us, the story of the beginning of your life and of my life and of the lives of all the other people in the world. That is why everybody is interested in it. We have all grown from eggs to babies and we have all been born.

And I can wish nothing better for you than that after you have grown up you may find someone whom you will love and who will love you and with whom you will have babies of your own. Then you will have lived the whole of the most wonderful of all stories, the story of how we become alive, and are born, and grow up.

95